Steck-Vaughn

WORLD MYTHS

The Adventures of Anansi

Reviewer
Abdullahi A. Ibrahim
Fellow, Institute for the Advanced Study and Research
of the African Humanities, Northwestern University

STECK-VAUGHN
COMPANY
A Subsidiary of National Education Corporation

ISBN 0-8114-3368-4

2 3 4 5 6 7 8 9 0 SEC 99 98 97

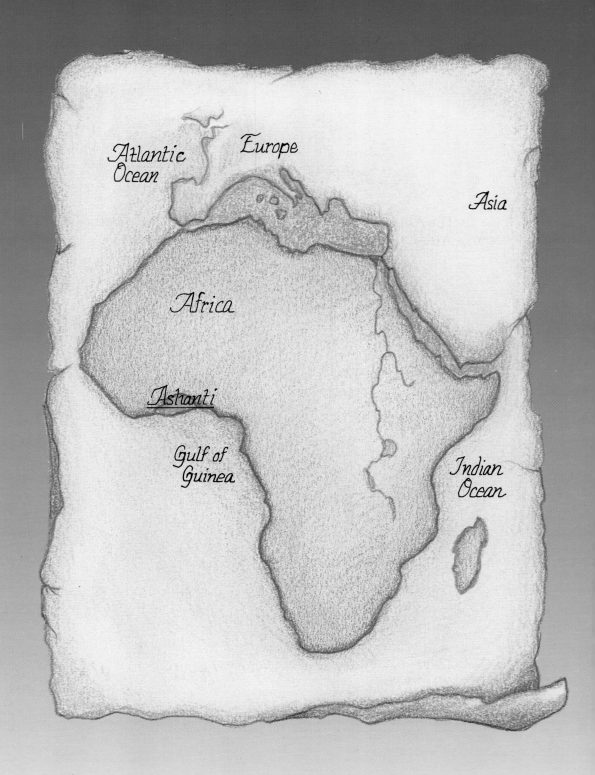

Atlantic
Ocean

Europe

Asia

Africa

Ashanti

Gulf of
Guinea

Indian
Ocean

Introduction

The Ashanti (uh SHAN tee) people live in several countries of West Africa. Look at the map on page 2 to see where they live. One of their favorite story characters is the spider they call Anansi (uh NAN see). Stories about Anansi came from Africa to the Americas when the Ashanti and other African people were brought here as slaves. Today people in the United States still tell stories about him, often calling him Annancy, Nancy, or Aunt Nancy. Such stories are also told in Jamaica and other islands in the Caribbean.

Anansi is a type of story character called a trickster. Sometimes tricksters are human in form, but more often they are animals. Anansi and other tricksters often appear in traditional stories called folktales. Although it is not always easy to tell the difference between folktales and myths, folktales are usually told for entertainment rather than for education. Myths are usually more serious stories in which divine beings may appear and the values of a culture may be explained.

In the myth here, Anansi is the great god's adviser—and even rival. But that doesn't make him less funny! As you read the story, see if you can figure out why Anansi is always called a trickster.

The Adventures
of Anansi

In West Africa the spider called Anansi (uh NAN see) is the cleverest of all the animals. After all, who else but Anansi can spin fine and complicated webs? Who else can catch prey in invisible, silken traps? In fact, people say that the great god of the heavens was so taken with the little fellow's cleverness that he appointed Anansi to be his chief advisor. After that, Anansi lived near the great god and made himself very useful.

One day the spider took a good look around the heavens and decided that the great god needed some help. So he went to the great god and asked him for an ear of corn.

"You may certainly have one," said the great god to his little advisor, "but what are you going to do with it?"

"I thought I'd go down to Earth and trade it for a troop of one hundred fine young people," Anansi boldly replied. "Then I'll bring them back to serve you. It seems to me that you could use some extra help up here in the heavens."

"You're right about that," said the great god, chuckling. "For the life of me, though, I can't figure out how you're going to use one little ear of corn to persuade one hundred people to come up here."

"Just you wait, great god!" replied the spider, dancing with delight. "Just you wait!"

"I'll be watching," said the great god, as he handed over the corn.

With the corn tied to his back, Anansi scuttled off down to Earth. At the first village he came to, he marched right up to the chief's door.

"I surely would be grateful for a night's lodging," Anansi said to the chief. "Oh—and I need a safe place to hide my ear of corn. You see, it belongs to the great god of the heavens, who would be terribly angry if it got lost."

The chief was happy to entertain the great god's advisor and showed him a hole in the roof of his hut that was just right for hiding the corn.

Soon the village settled down for the night, and Anansi could hear everyone snoring. He tiptoed on his eight little feet right up to the place where the corn was hidden. Dragging it outside, the tricky spider scraped off the kernels and fed them to the village chickens.

You can imagine what happened the next morning when Anansi learned that the great god's corn had disappeared in the night! He rushed about in a frenzy, hurling things into the air as he pretended to search for the corn.

"Disappeared?" he screeched. "Disappeared? What do you mean, disappeared? You mean stolen! Someone has stolen the corn of the great god! And he will hear about it, too, unless you give me something to make up for it!"

The eight-legged trickster made such a fuss that the chief gave him a large basket of corn just to get rid of him. Entertaining the great god's chief advisor was not easy!

Away Anansi went, dragging the heavy basket behind him. He did not get very far before he had to rest. As he sat panting by the side of the road, who should he see but a man with a fat chicken tucked under his arm.

"Friend," called Anansi cheerfully, "as the great god's chief advisor, I am preparing a feast up in Heaven. I need a fine chicken like the one you're carrying. Will you exchange it for this corn?"

The man was happy to provide a chicken for the heavenly feast. He eagerly handed over his bird to the spider.

Anansi continued on his way—now leading the chicken—until he came to a second village. Once again, he approached the chief and asked to stay overnight.

"And while you're at it," added the spider, "find a safe place to keep this fine fowl. You see, it belongs to the great god, and I would suffer if anything happened to it."

The chicken was put securely in a coop for the night, and the whole village went to sleep—except, of course, for Anansi. The crafty spider sneaked out of his bed in the darkness and let himself into the chicken coop. There he killed his bird and buried it. He scattered its feathers in front of the chief's door.

In the morning Anansi pretended to faint when he heard that the chicken was gone. And when everyone began to look for it, Anansi was the one who found its feathers near the chief's house.

"I am astounded that you would treat the great god's chicken with such dishonor!" shouted Anansi. "You can be sure that he will hear about your deed—that is, unless you can find me a worthy replacement for that fine fowl!"

The whole
village begged for forgiveness
and quickly gathered together a small
herd of their finest sheep. To the great relief of
the people, Anansi not only accepted the sheep but set off
immediately on his journey.

At noon, as he watched his sheep grazing, Anansi spied a small procession of people winding its way along the road. They were carrying the body of a young man who had died far from home. They were taking him, they explained, back to his people for burial.

"Say no more!" said Anansi, puffing out his small chest importantly. "Return now to your homes. As the great god's chief advisor, I will take over your worthy task and carry this man to his people! And as a reward for your trouble, please take these sheep. I have no need for them."

The people were delighted to exchange their burden for such fine animals. Anansi lugged the body to a nearby village. There he begged the chief for a bed.

"This young man is the great god's favorite son," whispered the tricky spider. "He has had a tiring journey and is fast asleep. He needs a quiet hut all to himself."

The chief gladly agreed to the spider's request, thinking that it was a great honor to play host to the god's favorite son. That night, everyone, including Anansi, slept soundly.

Early the next morning, Anansi sent the chief's children to awaken the god's son. "He sleeps very soundly," warned the spider. "You may have to shake him a bit."

Anansi sat down to wait. After a few minutes the children returned, claiming that no amount of shaking would awaken the young man. Pretending great terror, the spider rushed off to the hut. At the sight of the body, he threw himself to the ground. Thrashing and wailing, he shrieked, "Your shaking has killed the great god's favorite son! Without a doubt he will punish me and your entire village for this deed!"

The people were terrified at the thought of the god's anger and added their wailing to Anansi's. After a bit, the spider stood up straight on his eight legs.

"I have a plan," he announced calmly. "First we will bury the great god's son. Then you must give me one hundred of your finest young people. I will take them with me to the heavens to bear witness to the great god that the chief's children, and not I, caused the death of his son. Since it was an accident, perhaps the great god will be merciful."

What else could the chief and his people do? They realized that nothing else would overcome the anger of the great god, so they did as Anansi advised.

And so, not long afterward, the great god of the heavens saw Anansi triumphantly leading a troop of one hundred strong young people down the road.

"You see?" asked the spider, bursting with pride, "I have done as I promised. I have exchanged your ear of corn for one hundred young people, all of whom are overjoyed to serve you."

"Well, Anansi," said the great god, laughing and shaking his head in amazement, "I never believed you could do it! I'm so pleased, I'll make you my commander in chief!"

After this, as you might imagine, there was no more living with Anansi. Everyone praised his deeds. Some even said he was as wise as the great god himself. Anansi was so pleased by their flattery that he began to believe it. Worse than that, he began to boast that he was even more clever than the great god!

When the great god heard this, he said to himself, "Anansi's head is much too big. I'll set him a task he'll never be able to accomplish. That will put him in his place!"

So the great god called the little spider to his high throne and, in his most terrible voice, thundered out his wishes. "Anansi, since you are so wise, I have an important task for you. I want you to find something and bring it back to me."

"Gladly, great god," replied the spider. "But what is that something you have in mind?"

"Exactly that," said the great god. "Something. What I have in mind will stay in mind."

"But how can I fetch something if I don't know what it is?" squeaked the spider in frustration.

"That, Anansi, is your problem. Go now, and don't come back without something." Then the great god threw back his head and made the heavens shake with his laughter. And poor Anansi scuttled away, tripping over his long legs in his confusion.

Back at home, Anansi sat down, crossed his many legs, and gathered his thoughts to try to solve his problem. How could he find something—what, he didn't know—and bring it back to the great god?

"Well, obviously," he said to himself, "I must first discover what something is. That will be the hard part. Once I know that, I can figure out how to get it."

Anansi paced and pondered and pondered and paced until he had formed a plan. Climbing down from the heavens, he set out on another journey across Earth. Every time he met a bird, he begged a beautiful feather from it. When he had one from every kind of bird on Earth, Anansi scampered back to the heavens and wove a many colored cloak from the feathers. Wrapping himself in this wonderful disguise, the little trickster perched on a tree branch outside the great god's window. When the great god looked out, he saw what appeared to be a brand-new sort of bird.

"H-mmm, what have we here? Some strange new bird! I surely didn't make it. I wonder who did?"

Puzzled, the great
god gathered everyone together and asked
them about the new bird in his tree. No one knew where it had
come from or what it was. As they marveled, someone shouted,
"Ask Anansi! Maybe he'll know!"

"Yes," everyone cried, "ask Anansi. Where is he?"

"Our spider friend is away," chuckled the great god. "He is
running a little errand for me—one that I think will show him his
place in the world."

The people forgot all about the new bird and asked the great god
what task he had set for Anansi this time.

"Well," he replied, "I have ordered him to fetch something for me."

"Yes, of course," said everyone, "but what exactly did you tell Anansi to bring you?"

"Nothing more than something," chortled the great god, obviously pleased with himself. "If Anansi is so clever, let him figure it out."

Everyone laughed heartily, delighted that the great god had outwitted his spider chief.

"But what exactly is this something?" someone insisted. "Now that Anansi is gone, you can tell us."

The great god rubbed his hands together in glee. "The something that I want our Anansi to bring me is the sun, the moon, and darkness. That would be hard enough for him, even if he did know what I wanted!"

Huddled within his feathered cloak, the crafty little spider choked back a hoot of triumph. "No, great god," he thought to himself, "finding the answer to the riddle of something was the hard part. The rest is easy."

And so Anansi rushed back to his house, shed his wonderful cloak of feathers, and prepared for yet another journey. This time he went to the ends of the Earth to visit his friend Python, who knew all about the wonders of the world. From him Anansi learned where the sun, moon, and darkness lived. Then it was a simple matter for the spider to scoop them up, stuff them into his webbed bag, and drag them home.

The next morning, refreshed by a deed well-done and a good night's sleep, Anansi appeared with his bag before the throne of the great god.

"Well, Anansi," said the great god, putting on a solemn face, "have you brought me something in your bag?"

"Yes," replied the spider, "I have brought you something—the very something you desire!"

With that, Anansi flung open his bag, and out rushed darkness, which enveloped the entire Earth. Then the spider poked the moon out, and it gave off just enough light for people to make out shapes. Finally he turned his bag upside down, and the sun bounced out, startling everyone with its brightness. Those who had turned away or closed their eyes were able to see all that the sun made clear, but those who had looked right at the sun were blinded forever.

Anansi never did learn his proper place. But the consequence of his trickery was sad indeed, for he brought blindness into the world.

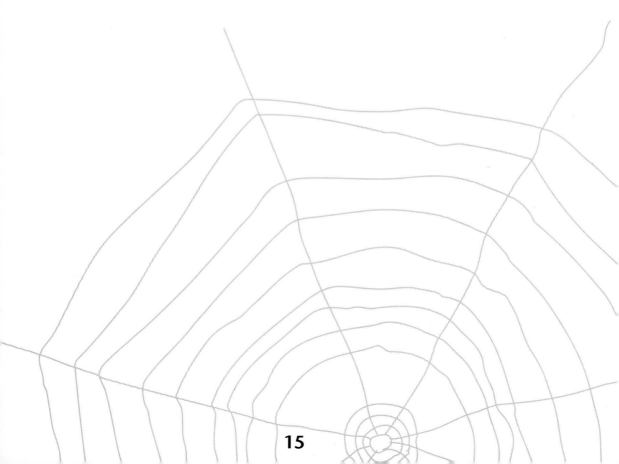

Glossary

adviser *n.* Person who gives someone else advice about how to handle things. p. 3

astounded *adj.* Shocked; very surprised. p. 7

bear witness *v.* To act as proof or evidence that something is true. p. 9

burial *n.* Act of placing a dead body in a grave or tomb. p. 8

dishonor *n.* Lack of respect. p. 7

divine *adj.* Having to do with a god; sacred; holy. p. 3

envelop *v.* To surround something completely. p. 15

replacement *n.* Something that takes the place of something else. p. 7

trickery *n.* Act of tricking or fooling others. p. 15

trickster *n.* A character in myths and stories who plays tricks on others and is mischievous. p. 3

Acknowledgments

Steck-Vaughn Company

Executive Editor Diane Sharpe
Senior Editor Martin S. Saiewitz
Assistant Art Director Cynthia Ellis

Proof Positive/Farrowlyne Associates, Inc.

Program Development, Design, and Production

Illustration

Marcy Ramsey